I dedicate this book to my best friend, my father
Giuseppe, who instilled in me courage, strength,
and the determination to never give up.
I love you daddy

Spagetata

🍴 4-6 servings   🕐 30 minutes

INGREDIENTS

1/2 Cup extra virgin olive oil

1/4 Chopped garlic

1 lbs Spaghetti

2 Cups Chopped basil

2 Cups Chopped parsley

4 Cups Cherry tomatoes

4 Slices of anchovies

1/4 Teaspoon Crushed red pepper

Salt and pepper to taste

DIRECTIONS

- Add oil to sautéed pan
- Melt down anchovies in pan
- Add garlic until lightly golden
- Add cherry tomatoes
- Cook tomatoes until they soften up
- Then crush them down
- Cook sauce on low flame for 15 min
- Add salt and pepper to taste
- Cook spaghetti as directed on box
- Make sure to salt your pasta water generously
- Drain pasta when cooked
- Pour pasta in the pan with the sauce
- Mix well until all combined
- Add basil and parsley
- Toss all together
- Add grated cheese if desired

ENJOY!

Chickpea Pasta

🍴 4-6 servings   🕐 30 minutes

INGREDIENTS

1/2 Cup chopped onion

5 Cloves chopped garlic

1/4 Cup extra virgin olive oil

3 19oz Can of chickpea (2 drained 1 not drained)

1 Ibs Ditali pasta

1/2 Teaspoon rosemary

2 Dry bay leaves

2 cups water

2 Inch rind of parmesan cheese

1 cup grated pecorino romano cheese

Salt and pepper to taste

DIRECTIONS

- Place oil in pan
- Add onions
- Sauté onions until translucent
- Add garlic, saute lightly
- Add chickpeas, rosemary, and bay leaves.
- Add salt and pepper to taste
- Add water
- Add parmesan cheese rind
- Bring to a boil and let simmer for 15 min
- Use immersion blender and pulse a few times
- Cook pasta as directed on box (Make sure to add salt to water)
- Drain pasta reserving 1 cup of pasta water
- Pour the pasta into the chickpea mixture
- Add the 1 cup of reserved pasta water
- Add pecorino romano cheese
- Cooke 2 more minutes while constantly stirring
  ENJOY!

Spaghetti with garlic and oil

🍴 4-6
servings

🕐 15
minutes

INGREDIENTS

1 lbs Spaghetti
6 Cloves sliced garlic
1 Cup extra virgin olive oil
8 Slices of anchovies
1/4 Teaspoon crushed red pepper
2 Cups fresh parsley
3 Parsley stems
Salt and pepper to taste

DIRECTIONS

- Add oil to large pan
- Add anchovies
- Cook until melted down
- Add parsley stems, garlic, crushed red pepper, salt and pepper to taste and sauté until garlic is lightly golden.
- Turn off the flame
- Cook pasta as directed on box (Make sure to add salt to water)
- Drain pasta and reserve 1 cup of pasta water
- Pour into pan with sauce
- Turn on heat
- Add pasta water
- Add fresh parsley
- Toss all together
- Cook 2 more minutes until everything mixes well
- Add cheese if desired
  ENJOY!

Spaghetti with spicy red crab sauce

 6-8 servings   60 minutes

INGREDIENTS

10 Blue crabs
1/2 Cup chopped garlic
1 Cup and a 1/2 white wine
1/2 Cup fresh parsley
1 Teaspoon crushed red pepper
2 28oz cans of tomato pure`
28 oz Water
Salt and pepper to taste
1 1/12 lbs Spaghetti
1/2 Cup extra virgin olive oil

DIRECTIONS

- Add crabs to large pot
- Sauté for 5 min
- Add oil
- Add garlic
- Sauté garlic until lightly golden
- Add wine
- Sauté for 3 min with wine
- Add parsley
- Add crushed red pepper
- Add sauce
- Add water
- Add salt and pepper to taste
- Let cook for 1 hour while stirring occasionally
- Cook spaghetti following box directions (Make sure to add salt to the water)
- Remove crabs and put aside
- Drain spaghetti and pour into sauce pan
- Mix all together
  ENJOY!

fusilli with pesto

🍴 4-6 servings   🕐 15 minutes

INGREDIENTS

2 Cups fresh basil

1 Cup extra virgin olive oil

1/2 Cup walnuts

4 Cloves of garlic

1/2 Cup pecorino romano cheese

Salt and pepper to taste

1 lbs Fusilli pasta

DIRECTIONS

- Blend basil, oil, garlic, walnuts, cheese and salt and pepper
- Cook pasta as directed on box (Make sure to add salt to the water)
- Drain pasta while reserving 1 cup of pasta water
- Place pesto sauce in large bowl
- Add drained pasta
- Add pasta water
- Toss all together ENJOY!

Pasta with lemon ricotta

🍴 4-6 servings   🕐 15 minutes

INGREDIENTS

1 lb any shaped pasta

2 Cups Fresh ricotta

1 Cup pecorino romano grated cheese

Zest of 1 lemon

1/2 of a squeezed lemon

Salt and pepper to taste

1/2 Cup pasta water

DIRECTIONS

- In large bowl add ricotta, pecorino romano, lemon zest, lemon juice and salt and pepper
- Mix well
- Cook pasta as directed (Make sure to add salt to the water)
- Drain pasta while reserving 1/2 cup of pasta water
- Pour drained pasta into bowl with mixture
- Add reserved pasta water
- Toss well all together ENJOY!

Paccheri with whiskey cream sauce

 4-6 servings   🕐 20 minutes

INGREDIENTS

1/2 Cup extra virgin olive oil

2 Chopped shallots

Pinch of crushed red pepper

1 Small can of tomato paste (6 oz)

1/4 Cup of whiskey

2 Cups heavy cream

Salt and pepper to taste

1 lb paccheri pasta

1 Cup of pecorino romano cheese

DIRECTIONS

- In large pan add olive oil
- Add shallots
- Sauté until translucent
- Add crushed red pepper
- Add tomato paste
- Cook tomato paste for 3 minutes
- Add whiskey
- Cook for 2 minutes
- Add heavy cream
- Add salt and pepper to taste
- Cook all together for 5 more minutes
- Cook pasta as directed on box (Make sure to add salt to the water)
- Drain cooked pasta
- Pour into sauce
- Add pecorino romano
- Toss all together
  ENJOY!

Lemon Butter Sage pasta

🍴 4-6 servings   🕐 15 minutes

INGREDIENTS

1 Stick salted butter
3 Fresh sage leaves
Salt and pepper to taste
1 lb any shaped pasta
1/2 Cup of pasta water
Zest of 1 lemon
Juice of 1 lemon
1 Cup pecorino romano cheese

DIRECTIONS

- In large pan add butter, sage leaves, the zest and lemon juice, and salt and pepper
- Let cook until all butter is melted
- Cook pasta as directed (Make sure to add salt to water)
- Drain pasta while reserving pasta water
- Pour drained pasta in butter sauce
- Toss all together while adding reserved pasta water
- Add cheese
- Toss all together ENJOY!

Calamarata

 4-6 servings   30 minutes

INGREDIENTS

1 lbs calamari shaped pasta

1/2 Cup extra virgin olive oil

3 Parsley stems

4 Cloves of fresh garlic

2 lbs Fresh cut up calamari

2 Cups cherry tomatoes

1 Cup fresh chopped parsley

Salt and pepper to taste

1 Cup white wine

DIRECTIONS

- In large skillet add oil, parsley stems, and garlic
- Sauté for a couple of minutes
- Add calamari
- Add salt and pepper
- Remove parsley stems
- Cook calamari for 5 minutes and remove
- Add cherry tomatoes
- Add parsley
- Add salt and pepper
- Cook tomatoes for 8 min
- Add white wine
- Cook for another 5 min with the wine
- Add calamari back to the skillet
- Cook another 2 min all together
- Cook pasta as directed (Make sure to add salt to water)
- Drain pasta and add to skillet with calamari
- Toss all together
- Add fresh parsley on top
  ENJOY!

Spaghetti With Fried Zucchini

🍴 4-6 servings   🕐 30 minutes

INGREDIENTS

4 Sliced zucchini in disc form
1 lb spaghetti
1 1/2 Cups extra virgin olive oil
Salt and pepper to taste

DIRECTIONS

- Add oil to large skillet
- Bring oil up to frying temperature
- Fry zucchini in one layer until golden brown and put salt and pepper to taste on every layer as you are frying
- Remove zucchini as they cook
- Cook pasta as directed on package
- Pour cooked pasta into skillet with the extra virgin olive oil
- Toss well all together
- Add all the fried zucchini on top

ENJOY!

Pasta with cauliflower and breadcrumbs

 4-6

servings

 30

minutes

INGREDIENTS

1 Head of raw cauliflower

1/2 Cup extra virgin olive oil

5 Slices anchovies

1 Cup chopped onion

1/2 Cup raisins

1/4 Cup pignoli nuts

Pepper to taste

1 Cup plain bread crumbs

1 Tablespoon

1 lbs Buccatini pasta

DIRECTIONS

- Boil cauliflower with salted water until fork tender
- Drain and put aside
- In large skillet put extra virgin olive oil
- Add anchovies
- Melt down anchovies for a couple of minutes
- Add onions
- Cook onions until translucent
- Add raisins
- Add pignoli nuts
- Add black pepper to taste
- Cook all together for 5 more minutes

Breadcrumb Topping:

-Place breadcrumbs in small skillet with sugar and 2 tablespoons of extra virgin olive oil

-Sauté for a few min until breadcrumbs become toasty

-Place aside

- Add cauliflower in sauce
- Break down the cauliflower in the sauce and cook all together for 10 min
- Add 1 cup pasta water in the sauce
- Cook pasta as directed (Add salt to water)
- Drain pasta
- Add to sauce
- Start tossing together until creamy
- Serve with breadcrumbs on top as desired

ENJOY!

Zitoni with Cherry Tomatoes and Tuna

🍴 4-6 servings   🕐 30 minutes

INGREDIENTS

4 Cups cherry tomatoes

2 Cans of Italian tuna in olive oil

1/4 Cup extra virgin olive oil

3 Fresh parsley stems

4 Cloves sliced garlic

1 lb Zitoni pasta

1/2 Freshly chopped parsley

1/2 Cup white wine

DIRECTIONS

- In large skillet, add oil
- Add parsley stems and garlic
- Sauté garlic for 2 minutes
- Add cherry tomatoes
- Cook cherry tomatoes for 5 minutes and crush them down
- Add salt and pepper to taste
- Remove parsley stems discard
- Add white wine
- Let cook for an additional 5 minutes
- Add cans of tuna
- Mix well
- Cook pasta as directed on the package (Don't forget to salt your water)
- Drain cooked pasta and toss in skillet with sauce
- Toss well and add fresh parsley

ENJOY!

Farfalle Alla Boscaiola

 4-6

servings

🕐 30

minutes

INGREDIENTS

1 lb Farfalle pasta

1 Pint of heavy cream

5 Large sliced portobello mushrooms

1 Mushroom bouillon

2 Cups pecorino romano cheese

1/2 Cup freshly chopped parsley

Salt and pepper to taste

1 Cup reserved pasta water

2 Cloves chopped garlic

DIRECTIONS

- In large skillet add oil
- Add sliced mushrooms
- Add pepper to taste
- Sauté mushrooms until nice and crispy
- Add garlic
- Cook for 1 minute
- Add parsley
- Add heavy cream, bouillon, and cook for 5 minutes
- Cook pasta as directed on package (Don't forget to salt your pasta water)
- Reserve 1 cup of pasta water
- Add cooked pasta into mushroom sauce
- Add grated cheese
- Toss all together until nice and creamy
- Add reserved pasta water if needed

ENJOY!

Rita's Lasagna

🍴 8-10 servings   🕐 3 Hours

INGREDIENTS

1/4 Cup extra virgin olive oil

1 Cup chopped onion

1/4 Cup chopped garlic

3 lbs Chopped meat

1 6oz Can tomato paste

1 28oz can of tomato pure

2 Seared pork ribs

4 Fresh basil leaves

Salt and pepper to taste

1 Box of no boil lasagna

1 lb sliced ham

1 lb sliced white American cheese

4 Cups of béchamel sauce

3 cups grated pecorino romano

2 Tbs sugar

DIRECTIONS

- In large pot add extra virgin olive oil
- Add onions
- Sauté for 2 minutes
- Add garlic
- Sauté for 1 minute
- Add chopped meat
- Crush chopped meat and cook until browned
- Add tomato paste
- Cook for 3 minutes
- Add tomato pure'
- Add 56oz of water
- Add pork ribs
- Add basil
- Add salt and pepper to taste
- Add sugar
- Cook sauce while stirring occasionally for 90 minutes
- In a baking pan, start the layering process with sauce, lasagna sheets, sauce, béchamel, ham, white American and grated cheese
- Repeat this process once more
- Top lasagna with sauce and grated cheese
- Place in a 425 degree oven for 30 minutes or until bubbly
- Let cool for 20 minutes before serving

Enjoy!

Bacon wrapped stuffed meatloaf with broccoli rabe

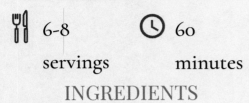

6-8 servings   **60** minutes

INGREDIENTS

2 Cups soaked, squeezed out bread

4 lbs Chopped meat

1/4 Cup chopped garlic

1 Finley chopped medium onion

1 Cup chopped fresh parsley

1 Cup pecorino romano grated

3 Eggs

1 Cup 4c Italian seasoned breadcrumbs

1 Package of bacon

Salt and pepper to taste

1/2 lbs sliced ham

1/2 lbs sliced provolone

1 1/2 Cup cooked broccoli rabe

DIRECTIONS

- In large bowl mix chopped meat, soaked bread, garlic, onion, parsley, cheese, eggs, breadcrumbs and salt and pepper
- Flatten out meat mixture on parchment paper into a large rectangular shape
- Place layer of ham
- Place layer of provolone
- Layer on the broccoli rabe
- Roll up meat mixture using the parchment paper to help you along
- Wrap in bacon
- Bake at 425 degrees until bacon is crispy and the meat is fully cooked ENJOY!

Italian shake and bake

🍴 4-6
servings

🕐 60
minutes

INGREDIENTS

12 Chicken legs
1/2 Cup extra virgin olive oil
1 Tablespoon of adobo seasoning
2 lbs Baby potatoes
4 Cups 4C bread crumbs
4 Leaves of fresh basil (Chopped)
1/4 Cup parsley (chopped)
1 Tablespoon rosemary (Chopped)
1 Tablespoon chives (chopped)
3 fresh bay leaves (chopped)
Salt and pepper to taste

DIRECTIONS

- In a plastic bag place chicken, half the oil and adobo
- Seal bag and shake well
- In another bag place breadcrumbs
- Put the chicken in the bag with the breadcrumbs and shake until all chicken is coated in breadcrumbs
- In another bag place potatoes, the other half of the oil, fresh herbs and salt and pepper (Shake until all potatoes are coated)
- Place chicken and potatoes in large baking pan
- Place in 425 degree oven until potatoes and chicken are fully cooked and crispy
  Enjoy!

Candied Acorn Squash

🍴 4-6
servings

🕐 60
minutes

INGREDIENTS

1 Large acorn squash sliced into wedges

1/2 Cup honey

1/2 Cup brown sugar

Salt and pepper to taste

1/4 Cup extra virgin olive oil

DIRECTIONS

- Place one layer of acorns on cooking sheet
- Drizzle with oil
- Season with salt and pepper
- Place in a 450 degree oven
- Cook for 40 minutes while flipping half way through
- Coat with honey and brown sugar on both sides and bake for an additional 20 minutes until nicely roasted

Beer Battered Fish

🍴 4-6 servings 🕐 30 minutes

INGREDIENTS

3 lbs Fresh fluke

1 Tablespoon old bay seasoning

3 Cups all purpose flour

1 1/2 Bottles of beer

2 cups canola oil

Salt to taste

DIRECTIONS

- In a bowl mix flour, half the old bay, and beer until batter is formed
- Season the fluke with the other half of old bay
- Place all the fish in batter while stirring gently until all coated
- In large pan place canola oil
- Bring oil temperature up for frying
- Gently place the beer bettered fish into the oil without over crowding the pan
- Flip fish when golden brown
- Remove fish when both sides are golden and put onto a wire rack
- Sprinkle with salt ENJOY!

Pork Steak Milanese with Cherry Peppers

🍴 6 servings 🕐 30 minutes

INGREDIENTS

6 Pork steaks

3 Cups 4c seasoned breadcrumbs

1 Cup pecorino romano cheese grated

1 1/2 Cup freshly chopped parsley

3 Eggs

2 Cups canola oil

1/4 Cup extra virgin olive oil

1/4 Cup chopped garlic

1 Cup pickled cherry peppers

1/2 Cup white wine

Salt and pepper to taste

1/4 Cup Italian dressing

DIRECTIONS

Pork Steaks:

- In a bowl add breadcrumbs, grated cheese, 1 cup of fresh parsley, salt and pepper to taste
- Mix well
- In another bowl add eggs, Italian dressing, salt and pepper
- Mix well
- Dip pork steaks in egg mixture, and then coat with breadcrumb mixture
- Place aside
- In a large skillet add canola oil
- Fry all pork steak until golden brown and place aside

Cherry Pepper Mixture:

- In a skillet add extra virgin olive oil and garlic
- Sauté garlic for 2 minutes
- Add cherry peppers, 1/2 cup of parsley, white wine, salt and pepper
- Cook for 5 minutes
- Pour cherry pepper mixture on top of pork steaks

ENJOY!

Potatoes and Eggs

🍴 4-6
servings

🕐 30
minutes

INGREDIENTS

5 Large sliced potatoes
6 Eggs
1 Cup chopped fresh parsley
1/2 Cup extra virgin olive oil
Salt and pepper to taste

DIRECTIONS

- In a bowl mix eggs, parsley, salt and pepper
- In large skillet, heat up olive oil
- Place potatoes in skillet
- Season with salt and pepper
- Cook potatoes until golden brown
- Add egg mixture onto potatoes
- Mix in all together until eggs are fully cooked
    Enjoy!

Meatball Stew

 4-6
servings

 60
minutes

INGREDIENTS

1 Cup soaked squeezed out bread
2 lbs Chopped meat
2 Tablespoons of grated onion
1/2 Cup pecorino romano
1/2 Fresh chopped parsley
2 Garlic cloves grated
1/2 Cup of 4c Italian seasoned
breadcrumbs
2 Eggs
Salt and pepper to taste
1 Cup canola oil
1/2 Cup extra virgin olive oil
1 Cup chopped onion
2 Cloves chopped garlic
1 Cup frozen peas
4 Cut up large potatoes
1 1/2 Cartons chicken broth
2 in Piece of parmesan rind

DIRECTIONS

- In a bowl mix soaked bread, chopped meat, onion, cheese, parsley, garlic, breadcrumbs, eggs, and salt and pepper
- Form desired sized balls out of meat mixture
- In a skillet add canola oil
- Sear all meatballs and place on the side
- In large pot add extra virgin olive oil
- Add onions and cook for 2 min
- Add chapped garlic
- Cook for 1 min
- Add peas
- Add salt and pepper
- Sauté for 3 min
- Add meatballs
- Add potatoes
- Add chicken broth
- Add parmesan rind
- Bring it up to a boil
- Bring flame down to medium low
- Cook until potatoes are fully cooked
      ENJOY!

Stuffed Artichokes

 6 servings 60 minutes

INGREDIENTS

6 Large artichokes

1 Lemon

6 Cups 4C bread crumbs

1/4 Crushed garlic

1 Cup fresh parsley

1 Cup pecorino Romano cheese

Salt and pepper to taste

1 Cup Cubed dry cheese

4 Cloves garlic

1/4 Cup olive oil

DIRECTIONS

- Prepare a large bowl filled with water with squeezed lemon in water
- Properly prep and clean artichoke to get it ready for stuffing
- In large bowl, mix together breadcrumbs , garlic, parsley, grated cheese and salt and pepper
- Open artichoke by spreading the leaves while packing in the breadcrumb mixture
- Sporadically stuff the dry cheese into the artichoke
- Place all stuffed artichokes in large pot, make sure they all fit nice and tight so they don't flip over
- Add water to pot with the water level reaching right below the rim of the artichoke
- Add the cloves of garlic in the water and season the water with salt
- Drizzle all the artichokes with extra virgin olive oil
- Cook artichokes covered until fork tender

Enjoy!

Fluke Francese

🍴 4 servings 🕐 30 minutes

INGREDIENTS

4 Large fillets of fresh fluke

3 Eggs

3 Tbs Italian dressing

1 1/2 Cups all purpose flour

1 Tsp Adobo seasoning

1/4 Cup extra virgin olive oil

3 Tbs butter

1 Tbs rinsed capers

1/2 Cup white wine

2 Cloves chopped garlic

The juice 3 lemons

1/2 Cup chopped parsley

Salt and pepper to taste

DIRECTIONS

- In a bowl mix eggs, Italian dressing, salt and pepper
- In a separate pan mix flour, salt, pepper and adobo
- In large skillet, add extra virgin olive oil and butter
- Drench fluke in flour first, then egg mixture, and then place in the hot oil in skillet
- Repeat with the rest of the fluke
- When golden brown remove fluke and place aside
- In the same skillet add garlic, wine, capers, lemon juice, parsley, salt and pepper
- Return fish into skillet and let it all cook together for 5 minutes

ENJOY!

Open Faced Stuffed Eggplant

 10

servings

 30

minutes

INGREDIENTS

2 Large sized eggplants

1/4 Cup extra virgin olive oil

2 Large very ripe tomatoes

2 Cups of soaked squeezed out bread

1 Cup 4c seasoned breadcrumbs

1/2 Cup pecorino romano grated cheese

1/2 Cup ripped fresh basil

1/4 Cup freshly chopped parsley

Salt and pepper to taste

DIRECTIONS

- Slice eggplant in half inch circles
- Place on cooking sheet
- Drizzle with extra virgin olive oil
- Season with salt and pepper
- Place in 425 degree oven for 15 minutes
- In large bowl mix together soaked bread, breadcrumbs, basil, cheese, chopped tomatoes, parsley and oil
- Add salt and pepper to taste
- Mix well all together
- Remove eggplants from oven
- Evenly distribute stuffing on top of each eggplant slice
- Drizzle with some olive oil
- Place back into 425 degree oven for an additional 15 minutes or until nicely toasted

ENJOY!

Rice balls

🍴 10   🕐 2 Days

servings

INGREDIENTS

4 1/2 Cups of rice

1 Tsp Saffron

1/2 Stick of butter

1 Tsp of chicken bullion

1/4 Cup extra virgin olive oil

1 Large chopped white onion

1/4 Cup chopped garlic

2 1/2 lbs Ground chuck

1 Small can of tomato paste

14 oz Tomato pure`

Salt and pepper to taste

1 tbs sugar

3 Eggs

1 tbs flour

3 Cups plain breadcrumbs

8 Cups of canola oil

DIRECTIONS

- In very large pot put 12 cups of water
- Salt the water to taste
- Bring the water to a boil
- Add rice, saffron, chicken bullion, butter and pepper to taste
- Boil rice until creamy and well done
- Wait until rice fully cools off
- In large pot add olive oil and onions
- Sauté onions for two minutes
- Add garlic
- Sauté for 1 minute
- Add ground chuck
- Cook until browned
- Drain out any excess grease
- Add tomato paste
- Add tomato pure`
- Add salt and pepper to taste
- Add 42 oz water
- Add sugar
- Cook for an hour and a half until sauce becomes very thick
- Let sauce fully cool down
- Before forming the balls prepare egg mixture with eggs, flour and salt and pepper to taste
- To form the balls place 1 cup of rice in your hand while forming a hole in the middle
- Fill hole with a couple of tablespoons of meat mixture
- Close the ball with your hands very firmly
- Roll rice ball in egg mixture coating all sides
- Then roll into plain bread crumbs
- Put aside
- In large pot bring canola oil up to frying temperature
- Place balls in oil and fry until golden brown and remove

Enjoy!

Potato Stuffed Peppers

🍴 10   🕐 2 Days

servings

INGREDIENTS

6 Colorful bell peppers

6 Cups of mashed potatoes

1/2 Stick of butter

2 Cups of sautéed peas with onion and garlic

2 Cups premosale cheese chopped

1 Cup fresh chopped parsley

1 Cup freshly chopped basil

2 Cups pecorino romano grated cheese

2 Eggs

Salt and pepper to taste

1 Cup plain panko breadcrumbs

1/2 Cup extra virgin olive oil

DIRECTIONS

- Slice pepper vertically in half, cleaning the inside out
- In a large bowl add mashed potatoes, peas, butter, premosale cheese, parsley, basil, 1 cup pecorino romano, eggs, salt and pepper
- Mix all ingredients well
- Stuff peppers with mixture, distributing evenly throughout all peppers
- Place stuffed peppers on a baking sheet
- Sprinkle grated cheese on top of the stuffed peppers
- Sprinkle panko breadcrumbs on top of peppers
- Drizzle extra virgin oil on top of peppers
- Cover and put in the oven at 425 degrees for 30 minutes then uncover for another 15 minutes
ENJOY!

Broccoli Rabe balls

🍴 4-6
servings

🕐 30
Minutes

INGREDIENTS

2 Cups of soaked and squeezed out
Italian bread
2 Cups cooked chopped broccoli
rabe
1/2 Cup Pecorino romano
1/2 Cup chopped fresh parsley
1 Cup 4C seasoned Italian
breadcrumbs
1 tbs Grated garlic
Salt and pepper to taste
2 Eggs
2 Cups canola oil

DIRECTIONS

- In large bowl mix in
  soaked bread, broccoli
  rabe, pecorino romano,
  chopped parsley,
  breadcrumbs, grated
  garlic, eggs, and salt and
  pepper to taste
- Form mixture into oval
  balls
- In large skillet bring
  canola oil to frying
  temperature
- Place formed balls in oil
  leaving space in
  between
- fry until golden brown
  Enjoy!

Candied carrots and brussels sprouts

🍴 4-6 servings 🕐 60 Minutes

INGREDIENTS

10 Carrots
1 lb Frozen brussels sprouts
1/4 Cup brown sugar
1/4 Cup honey
Salt and pepper to taste
3 Tbs extra virgin olive oil

DIRECTIONS

- In baking pan add carrots and brussels sprouts
- Toss with oil, salt and pepper
- Place in oven at 450 degrees for 30 minutes
- Add brown sugar and honey
- Toss well all together
- Continue cooking until vegetables are caramelized and tender Enjoy!

Escarole and Chickpea Soup

🍴 4-6
servings

🕐 60
Minutes

INGREDIENTS

2 Bunches of fresh escarole washed and chopped

1/4 Extra virgin olive oil

8 Whole cloves of garlic

1 Pint cherry tomatoes

4 Cans of drained chickpeas

1/4 Tsp crushed red pepper

2 Inch piece of parmesan cheese rind

2 Quarts chicken broth

Salt and pepper to taste

DIRECTIONS

- In large pot add olive oil
- Add garlic
- Cook for 2 minutes
- Add cherry tomatoes
- Cook for 7 minutes
- Crush cherry tomatoes down
- Add the escarole, chickpeas, parmesan rind, crushed red pepper, salt, pepper and chicken broth
- Cover and cook for 20 minutes
- Eat with crunchy bread ENJOY!

Pasta with Cucuzza

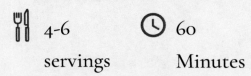

4-6 servings   **60** Minutes

INGREDIENTS

1 Extra long cucuzza pealed, clean and chopped

2 Cups cleaned and chopped cucuzza leaves

1 lb broken spaghetti in 1 inch pieces

1/4 Cup extra virgin olive oil

6 Cloves chopped garlic

1 Can pealed tomatoes (28oz)

5 Fresh basil leaves chopped

1 Chopped large white onion

Salt and pepper to taste

DIRECTIONS

- Fill large pot with water
- Add cucuzza, cucuzza leaves, onions, and salt to taste
- Bring it up to a boil and cook until cucuzza is tender
- In seperate skillet add extra virgin olive oil and garlic
- Cook garlic for 2 mintues
- Add pealed tomatoes, basil, salt and pepper
- Cook for 15 minutes while crushing down tomatoes
- Add pasta to the pot with the cucuzza
- Cook as directed on the box
- Drain out excess water while leaving some water in the pot to give it a soup consistency
- Add pealed tomatoes into the pot
- Stir it all together
    ENJOY!

Rice Salad

🍴 4-6 servings   🕐 10 Minutes

INGREDIENTS

6 Cups cooked rice
4 Cups chopped fresh
arugula
1/2 lb chopped fresh
prosciutto
1 Cup Mozzarella pearls
1 Cup cherry tomatoes
chopped in half
1 Cup cubed genoa salami
1/2 Cup sliced green olives
1/4 Cup chopped sundried
tomatoes in oil
1/4 Cup sliced pickled
pepperoncini
1/4 cup Sliced sweet
roasted peppers
1 Cup shaved parmesan
1 Cup fresh parsley
chopped
1 Cup chopped basil
2 tbs fresh chopped chives
1 Cup extra virgin olive oil
The juice of 5 squeezed
lemons
Salt and pepper to taste

DIRECTIONS

- In large bowl mix all ingredients together
- Serve and enjoy!

Gnocchi Tuna Salad

🍴 10-15
servings

🕐 10
Minutes

INGREDIENTS

2 Packages of cooked, boiled, and drained gnocchi
2 Cups sliced cherry tomatoes
1 Cup mozzarella pearls
1/4 Cup sliced red onion
1 Cup sliced kalamata olives
3 Cans of drained Italian tuna in oil
4 Cups fresh arugula
1/2 Cup chopped fresh parsley
1/2 Cup chopped fresh basil
Juice of 4 lemons
Salt and pepper to taste
1 Cup extra virgin olive oil

DIRECTIONS

- In large bowl mix all ingredients together
- Serve and enjoy!

Fancy Bean Salad

🍴 10-15 servings 🕐 10 Minutes

INGREDIENTS

1 Cup cooked cut string beans
1 Cup chickpeas
1 Cup white cannellini beans
2 Cups chopped celery
1/2 Cup sliced red onion
1 Cup sliced pepperoncini
1 Cup sliced radishes
1 Cup sliced red pepper
1 Cup oven roasted sliced almonds
1 Cup dry cranberries
1 Cup crumbled feta cheese

Dressing:

1 Cup extra virgin olive oil
1/2 Cup white balsamic vinegar
2 Tbs honey
1 Tbs yellow mustard
1 Grated clove of garlic
The zest of 1 orange
The juice of 1 orange
Salt and pepper to taste

DIRECTIONS

- In a jar mix all dressing ingredients and shake well until nice and smooth
- In large bowl mix all ingredients together
- Pour dressing on salad
- Mex everything together
- Serve and enjoy!

Amoglio

_____

🍴 4-6
servings

🕐 10
Minutes

INGREDIENTS

1/4 Cup chopped
garlic
1 Cup extra virgin
olive oil
1/2 Cup red wine
vinegar
1/2 Cup lemon
juice
2 Cups chopped
fresh parsley
1/4 tsp crushed
red pepper
Salt and pepper to
taste

DIRECTIONS

- In a mortar, place
garlic and salt and
crush into a paste
- Add the rest of
ingredients
- Mix well
- Serve on top of any
cooked protein or
enjoy as a dip with
fresh bread

Octopus Potato Salad

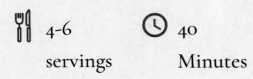

4-6 servings   40 Minutes

INGREDIENTS

1 6lb Fresh octopus
4 Boiled chopped potatoes
1 Cup chopped green olives
2 Cups chopped celery
1 Tbs crushed garlic
1/2 Cup chopped parsley
1/4 cup extra virgin olive oil
The juice of 3 lemons
Salt and pepper to taste
1 Whole lemon
2 Bay leaves

DIRECTIONS

- In large pot, put 1 1/2 gallons of water
- Squeeze the lemon and drop it in the water
- Add bay leaves
- Bring water up to a boil
- When water is boiling, hold octopus from the head and dip it in and out three times in boiling water
- Drop it in the water on the third dip
- Bring back up to a boil for 20 minutes
- Cover and shut off heat
- Let octopus sit in the water for a additional 20 minutes
- Remove octopus and chop it up into small pieces
- Place in a bowl with potatoes, olives, parsley, lemon juice, celery, garlic, olive oil, salt and pepper to taste.
- Toss well

ENJOY!

Lollipop Lamb Chops

🍴 6 servings 🕐 60 Minutes

INGREDIENTS

1 Cup extra virgin olive oil
4 Large sliced onions
21 Lollipop lamb chops
6 Sliced potato wedges
1 Tbs oregano
Salt and pepper to taste
1 Cup white wine

DIRECTIONS

- In large baking pan, place all ingredients and mix well
- Put in 450 degree oven for 60 minutes or until everything is cooked well

ENJOY!

Sweet Onion Mushroom Pizza

🍴 6 servings 🕐 20 Minutes

INGREDIENTS

1 Store bought pizza dough
2 Cups of caramelized onion
2 Cups sauté mushrooms
1 1/2 Cups fontina cheese
1/4 Cup extra virgin olive oil
Salt and pepper to taste

DIRECTIONS

- Lay out pizza dough on well greased baking sheet
- Add one layer of fontina cheese
- Add one layer of caramelized onions
- Add one layer of sautéed mushrooms
- Drizzle with extra virgin olive oil
- Add salt and pepper to taste
- Place in 425 degree oven for 20 minutes or until nice and crispy
  ENJOY!

Sausage and Broccoli Rabe Pizza

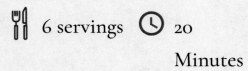 6 servings 🕐 20 Minutes

INGREDIENTS

1 Store bought pizza dough
1 Cup of gorgonzola cheese
2 Cups cooked, sautéed and chopped broccoli rabe
2 Cups cooked chopped sausage
1 Cup pecorino romano grated cheese
1/4 Cup extra virgin olive oil
Salt and pepper to taste

DIRECTIONS

- Lay out pizza dough on a finely greased pan
- Evenly add gorgonzola cheese
- Add broccoli rabe
- Add cooked sausage
- Add grated cheese
- Drizzle with oil
- Place in 425 degree oven for 20 minutes
    ENJOY!

Street Hotdog Pizza

🍴 6 servings 🕐 20 Minutes

INGREDIENTS

1 Store bought pizza dough
2 Cups cut up hotdogs
2 Cups of sweet hotdog onions
1/4 Cup extra virgin olive oil
Optional Toppings:
1 Cup sauerkraut
1 Cup relish
Ketchup
Mustard

DIRECTIONS

- Lay out pizza dough on a finely greased pan
- Evenly coat the dough with the onions
- Add hotdogs
- Drizzle with olive oil
- Place in a 425 degree oven for 20 minutes
- Remove from oven
- Add optional toppings if desired ENJOY!

Pizzalone

🍴 8 servings 🕐 30 Minutes

INGREDIENTS

2 Store bought pizza dough
2 Cups pizza sauce
1 lb shredded ham
2 Cups fresh ricotta
1/4 Cup extra virgin olive oil
2 Cups shredded mozzarella
Pepper to taste

DIRECTIONS

- Lay out first pizza dough on finely greased pan
- Put pizza sauce
- Add shredded ham
- Add ricotta
- Add mozzarella
- Add pepper
- Place the second pizza dough on top while sealing all edges
- Brush the top with extra virgin olive oil
- Make a few holes on top for venting
- Put in the oven at 425 degrees for 30 minutes
- Remove from oven and let it rest for 30 minutes before slicing
  ENJOY

Zeppoli

🍴 4-6 servings 🕐 10 Minutes

INGREDIENTS

4 Cups all
purpose flour
1 Tsp dry yeast
1 Tsp salt
1/4 Cup sugar
3 Cups very warm
water
6 Cups canola oil
1 Cup granulated
sugar
1 tbs ground
cinnamon

DIRECTIONS

- In a large bowl mix in flour, yeast, salt, sugar and warm water
- Stir well
- Cover bowl and place in warmest part in your home
- Let rest for 1 hour
- In large pot bring canola oil up to frying temperature
- With greased medium ice cream scooper, scoop batter and place in hot oil to fry
- Do not over crowd your pot
- Remove when golden brown and place in bowl with mixed sugar and cinnamon
- Toss well
  Enjoy!

Tiramisu

🍴 8-10 servings   🕐 24 hours

INGREDIENTS

9 Demitasse cups of espresso
3/4 Cup of Kaloah
1 1/3 Cups of sugar
1 lb Mascarpone cheese
3 Cups whipped cream
36 Lady finger cookies
1 Tbs coco powder

DIRECTIONS

- In bowl mix espresso, half a cup of kaloah and 1/3 cup of sugar
- Mix well
- In a bowl add cream, half a cup of sugar and whip well until it forms peaks
- In a bowl mix mascarpone cheese, half a cup of sugar
- Add whipped cream
- Fold together well
- Add 1 tbs kaloah and fold in
- In a tray, drizzle a few tablespoons of kaloah at the bottom
- Dunk lady fingers in espresso getting them very soaked and make your first layer at the bottom of the pan using half the lady fingers
- Spread out half of the cream mixture covering first layer of lady fingers
- Place another layer of soaked lady fingers on top using the rest of them
- Place the rest of the cream on top evenly
- Sprinkle with coco powder
- Chill for 24 hours

Enjoy!

Lemon Blueberry Upside down Cake

 8-10
servings

 50
minutes

INGREDIENTS

1 Lemon box cake
1 Blueberry box cake
4 Eggs
1 1/4 Cups of water
1/2 Cup vegetable oil
zest of 1 lemon
1 Tsp lemon extract
2 Pints fresh
blueberries
1/4 Cup granulated
sugar
1 Tbs powdered sugar

DIRECTIONS

- Line a 12 inch spring pan with parchment paper
- Pour sugar evenly on top of parchment paper
- Pour blueberries on top of sugar
- In a mixing bowl, mix together both cake mixes, eggs, oil, lemon zest, and lemon extract
- Mix well to create smooth batter
- Pour batter onto blueberries
- Place in the oven at 350 degrees for 50 minutes or until fully cooked
- Remove from spring pan and flip over onto cake dish
- Let it fully cool down and sprinkle with powdered sugar on top and enjoy

Fresh Ricotta

 10-15 servings   30 Minutes

INGREDIENTS

1 Gallon whole milk
1 quart heavy cream
1/2 Cup white vinegar
1 Tbs salt
1 Tbs sugar

DIRECTIONS

- In large pot, add milk, heavy cream, sugar and salt
- Bring up to a boil
- Lower to simmer for 5 minutes
- Shut heat
- Add vinegar
- Start stirring very slowly as ricotta floats to the top and separates from the curd
- Start removing ricotta with a skimmer
- Place in a drainable colander
- Let ricotta drain for a minimum of 30 minutes

Enjoy!

Sicilian Cream Puuffs

 10-15 servings   30 Minutes

INGREDIENTS

1 Stick of butter
1 Cup water
1/2 Tsp salt
1 Cup flour
5 Eggs
3 Cups of my fresh ricotta (Recipe on previous page)
1/2 Cup sugar plus 1 tsp
8 oz Mascarpone
1 Cup heavy cream whipped
3 Drops of cinnamon oil

DIRECTIONS

- In a pot add butter, water, salt and a half a teaspoon of sugar
- Melt down the butter
- Add flour
- Stir continuously until it forms into a dough and absorbs all liquids
- Add mixture into a bowl
- With electric mixture, start adding eggs one by one
- When all mixed together, scoop out a tablespoon amount of mixture onto cooking sheet using it all up
- Put them in a 420 degree oven for 30 minutes
- Remove from oven and let cool

Filling:

 – In a bowl add ricotta, mascarpone, sugar, whipped cream and cinnamon oil

 – Mix well

- Cut cream puffs in half
- Fill with 2 tablespoons of filling
- Sprinkle with powdered sugar
Enjoy!

Poor Mans Dessert

🍴 4-6 servings   🕐 20 Minutes

INGREDIENTS

1 Loaf of day old
Italian bread
4 Eggs
1 Tsp of vanilla
extract
3 Cups of milk
2 Cups canola oil
1 Cup of sugar
1 Tbs cinnamon

DIRECTIONS

- Cut Italian bread in one inch slices
- In small bowl add eggs and vanilla
- Mix well
- Add milk to another bowl
- Dunk bread in milk first and then in the egg mixture
- Place aside
- In large skillet add oil and bring up to frying temperature
- Add soaked bread in frying oil
- Cook until golden brown
- In another bowl mix sugar and cinnamon
- Place hot fried bread in the bowl with the sugar mixture
- Toss all together until well coated

ENJOY!

Easy Cassata

🍴 8 servings 🕐 40 Minutes

INGREDIENTS

3 Cups of my fresh ricotta
1 Cup sugar
3 Drops cinnamon oil
3/4 Cup Mini chocolate chips
2 Store bought pie crust
1 Tbs butter
1 Tbs powdered sugar
1 Tbs melted butter

DIRECTIONS

- In a bowl mix ricotta, sugar, cinnamon oil, and chocolate chips
- Using a pie pan, grease well with 1 tablespoon of butter
- Place one pie crust on the bottom
- Fill pie crust with ricotta mixture
- Make sure you flatten the ricotta evenly
- Place the second pie crust on top while pinching it closed all around the edges
- Make four 1 inch cuts in the middle of pie
- Brush the top with melted butter
- Place in 350 degree oven for 40 minutes
- Wait until it cools off and sprinkle with powdered sugar
- Refrigerate and eat cold ENJOY!

Pistachio Tiramisu

🍴 8-10 servings   🕐 24 Hours

INGREDIENTS

9 Demitasse cups of espresso
36 Lady finger cookies
1 Cup of pistachio liquor (and 1 Tbs)
2 Cups whipped cream
2 Cups pistachio pudding
2 Tbs pistachio cream spread
1 Cup of chopped pistachios

DIRECTIONS

- In a bowl mix whipped cream, pudding, pistachio cream spread, and a tablespoon of pistachio liquor
- Mix well and place aside
- In a another bowl add espresso and half a cup of pistachio liquor
- Mix well
- In a tray pour half a cup of pistachio liquor
- One by one, dunk half of the lady fingers in the espresso mixture and layer them on the bottom of the pan
- Spread half of the cream mixture covering the first layer of lady fingers
- Place another layer of soaked lady fingers on top using the rest of them
- Place the rest of the cream on top evenly
- Sprinkle with chopped pistachios
- Chill for 24 hours
    ENJOY!

Rita's Easy Lemon Ricotta cookies

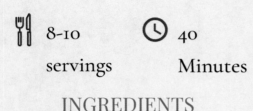 8-10 servings   🕐 40 Minutes

INGREDIENTS

1 Lemon store bought cake mix
1 Egg
15oz Whole milk fresh ricotta
1/2 Cup rainbow sprinkles
Icing:
2 Cups powdered sugar
2 Tbs lemon juice

DIRECTIONS

- In a bowl finely mix cake mix, ricotta, and egg until smooth
- With and ice cream scooper, scoop out batter and place on cooking sheet
- Place in the oven at 350 degrees for 15 minutes
- Remove from oven and let cool

Icing:

- In a bowl add powdered sugar and lemon juice
- Stir well until icing forms
- Dip top of cookie in icing and sprinkle with rainbow sprinkles immediately ENJOY!

Puff Pastry Almond Cookies

🍴 24 servings 🕐 30 Minutes

INGREDIENTS

1 Store bought puff pastry sheet
8oz Almond paste
1/4 Cup sugar
2 Tbs flour
2 Eggs
1 Tsp Vanilla extract
2 Tbs powdered sugar
1/4 Cup sliced almonds

DIRECTIONS

- While sprinkling some flour on a flat surface, lay out your puff pastry
- With a rolling pin, roll out creases in puff pastry
- In electric mixing bowl add almond paste, sugar, flour, vanilla extract and 1 egg
- Mix until smooth
- Place mixture and spread evenly onto puff pastry dough
- Vertically fold both sides of puff pastry meeting in the center
- Fold vertically one more time to form one log
- Slice log in half inch thick slices
- Pinch close and place on baking sheet
- Brush cookies with egg and sprinkle with sliced almonds
- Place in 400 degree oven for the first 15 minutes and lower oven to 350 for an additional 5 minutes
- Let cool and top with powdered sugar

ENJOY1

Made in the USA
Las Vegas, NV
18 November 2024

11609936R00062